ON YOUR LEFT

POEMS BY PEGGY BARNETT

To Edward,

It's been many years —
and a long journey. I hope
you enjoy these poems. They
are a special gift to a very
special person in my life!
I think we actually understand
each other — a rare thing indeed.
May we have many more years
of love —   your sister,

Peggy

CLARA BEAR PUBLISHING

First Edition, 2012
ISBN: 978-0-9858292-0-9
Printed and bound in the USA

Photography by Peggy Barnett
prbarnett.com

Layout and cover design by Emma Barnett
therealemmabarnett.com

Clara Bear Publishing 2012
Portland, OR

For my daughter, Emma

CONTENTS

PREFACE

There is a Latin name for it: *horror vacui* or "fear of empty space." Imagine living your whole life in New York City apartments (or lofts) with neighbors never more than twenty feet away from you both above, below and sideways, and then, at the age of sixty, suddenly finding yourself in a house on an acre of green ferns and foot trees, with neighbors' lights twinkling through the leaves far away in the darkness. There are alpacas across the road, horses down the lane and sheep around the corner. Little living things are always being eaten by coyotes—so at first you have bunnies running across the driveway at night lit up by your headlights, then you don't.

I was born in 1945 and grew up in Queens, New York. I went to Public School 89, Joseph Pulitzer JHS 145, Music and Art High School and to The Cooper Union and received a degree in Fine Art. After starving as an artist I opened Barnett Studio and became a very successful still-life and portrait photographer. I worked with my husband Ron for 45 years, then sold the studio in 2004. We moved north of Seattle to Maltby, Washington when my daughter Emma went off to college in Portland, Oregon.

The first dark night in my new home was a sleepless *horror vacui*. Soon after dawn I heard a "woosh-pop! woosh-pop!" over the house. In my nightgown I went out on the deck (the first deck of my life) and looked up to see a hot air balloon right overhead. The sun was shining through the silk glowing red and yellow. The people in the basket looked down, waving to me. I waved back. I knew I was in for a very different life.

Still, the furies of the past haunted me. Memories of the damage done to my family by the Holocaust, growing up Jewish in an Italian and Irish neighborhood, public school in the fifties, my mother-in-law's suicide, the trauma of seeing people falling out of the World Trade Center before it collapsed and the shock of the woman landing next to me on the sidewalk after jumping off a twelve-story building kept resurfacing.

So I turned from photography to an old love of mine, poetry. I still wander around beautiful Washington State taking landscape photographs, but mostly I write poetry. It has been a wonderful way to meet people—poets are great people. They are real people. They listen, they don't judge, and they have given me a haven of friendship in a new world. I thank you all for embracing a cranky, quirky poet who needs an audience within twenty feet of her, lest she feel alone.

THE LONGEST WORD

It was in the school yard of PS 89, Queens, in 1955
that I first heard the longest word of my life:
"antidisestablishmentarianism."
Ralph Hammelbacher said it fastest:
"antidisestablishmentarianism"
and we each repeated it ourselves
amazed at our brilliance;
at our ability to so conquer the English language.

"Antidisestablishmentarianism"
we whipped out the word
while sitting at the soda parlor counter
the jukebox playing Bing Crosby singing
"Would you like to swing on a star?"
as we ate the scrumptious banana splits
Mr. Wolke concocted
out of his homemade ice cream
the secret recipe for which he
bought with him from Vienna
after the War.
He never put his bananas in the refrigerator
"No, no, no no, no, no, no."
They melted, sweet and ripe
under the vanilla scented whipped cream.

I rolled it out again quickly
trippingly on my tongue
"antidisestablishmentarianism."
But it wasn't bigger than the
word we had learned yesterday in science:
"Hydrogen."
That word was really scary, because it was
followed by the small word:
"bomb."

BERRY MEMORIES

Blackberries squash under my tires on the driveway
purple blood
seeds on the concrete.
I have learned to embrace them,
as I have learned to embrace old age
and the astounding will of life to march on.
Blueberries, blackberries, wild strawberries
clusters of memories still remain hidden
only to be suddenly discovered
on the runners of my mind.

That summer
while Tante Putsi is busy polishing her doorknobs
my father decides to take me blueberry picking
in the fields near Peekskill, New York.
He parks the black 1949 Pontiac Sedan
by the side of the road
the sun glaring off its shiny fenders.
It's hot inside
smelling like an old sofa.
Below a quiet sunlit no cloud sky
flickering sweet smells grow high around me.
I feel lost.
Seeing a mound a few feet ahead of us
he picks up his little girl and puts her onto it
so she can reach the round blue fruits hanging above.
Daddy's fedora bobbing towards the ground
eat one, pick one
eat one, pick one
the happy rhythm of childhood work.
The tickling begins on my ankles
gradually reaching my knees.
Then the tickling is in my underpants
moving black on my arms.

I begin to scream.
The anthill has mobilized its invading armies.
Swung up in the air kicking and crying
trying to knock them off with my feet,
I'm carried, terrified,
under my father's arm to the Pontiac.
Thrown down on the burning oven's hood,
there follows lots of slapping, whipping, blowing
personal scratching out
and a strip search.
Exhausted, hopefully ant free
I'm returned to Tante Putsi
who makes me swim in Lake Peekskill
so I don't dirty the bath tub.

Two snails
their pseudopodia tackily pressed together
mate in the damp soil amongst the wild strawberries
in the green glaciered mountains
behind Hallstadt in the Austrian Alps.
White clouds are below us
long floating cotton puffs obscuring parts of the lake
wisps caught on medieval church spires.
The dark damp Grimm creatured forest surrounds us.
My mother had said
"Don't forget to eat the wild strawberries."
It was the only thing she said
when I told her we were visiting Austria
the home the Nazis took away from her.
She had nothing else to say.
On my knees in the black moist earth
I pick a tiny wild strawberry off a runner
put its bright green cap between my fingertips
pop it into my mouth.

The whole world becomes that strawberry.
I now know what my mother was
trying to tell me.
I now know what she had lost
what she had left behind.

I love jogging here in August.
All the way up to Maltby Road there are blackberries.
I jog, I eat
I jog, I eat
blackberries a reward for remembering.

A ROSE IS NOT A ROSE

I am turning my art into a rose garden
overturning my soil
toes curling into the fertilizer
soft from the pungent smell of alpacas.
I turn my poems into soft blooms
that would smell as sweet as the odor of decay
on a rainy day.
I can't wait to show you
the orange Vavooms
the golden Julia Childs
the scar on my leg where I fell into the
red Victory roses grown large
that bled down my leg
into the dirt.
I will come to you with armfuls
of sweet wine roses
brimming over
trailing behind me on the stone path
I am walking that leads away
and if I'm successful, back.
I am no longer young Rose Red
the outspoken and cheerful sister.
I peer suspiciously behind every bush
defended by thick green thorns.

Roses
another damn allegory of life and death.
For God's sake don't bloom into another poem
or morbid image.
You can live and die on your own.
Frankly
it's your good fortune to not know that
after each winter you will bloom again.

Or not.

WOLKE'S SODA PARLOR

On a Monday afternoon
I'm making ice cream with soft, ripe peaches.
Handel's Tenth Concerto Grosso
winds through the stems of
crisp yellow daffodils in a blue glass vase.
The ice cream is cold and sweet.
It reminds me of Wolke's Soda Parlor.

I am fourteen,
working at my first real job.
The soda parlor is on 90th Street
two blocks from my mother's sewing factory.
Using an old, secret Viennese recipe
Mr. Wolke churns his own ice cream
out of fresh fruit and walnuts
unhomogenized thick cream
and deep flavors that
melt into the sodas I make all summer.
My mother
who had obtained this job for me
with her own Viennese accent
always orders a coffee soda with maple-walnut ice cream.
It's Emma's favorite flavor,
a gene from her unknown grandmother.

One hot summer day
I'm standing behind the black marble counter
in my gray waitress uniform
wooden ceiling fans blowing my hair
leaning on my hands
sunlight streaming in the open door
forming a white rhomboid on the black granite floor.
A rumpled man in a shiny, gray suit
with the pained expression of heartburn

lowers his hot, wrinkled bottom
on the red, circular leather stool.
Eight fat fingers grip my counter
"Gimme a Bromo."
I reach behind me into a glass jar
to open a gray foil packet filled with grainy powder.
I invert it into an empty Coke glass
grab a second glass
fill it half full of water
then pour it into the first glass.
Back and forth I pour the frothing mix
bubbles skittering on my skin.
I hand it to him.
He drinks down it in breathless gulps.
After emitting a deep loud belch
he smiles, gently.
"Five cents, please."
"Sure sweetheart, here's a dime. Keep the change."
He struts out.
Yes, it's just like the old B/W movies,
and I'm the sweetie.

The cook is a big square Greek named Tulle.
He punishes his sons with a leather belt
strapping them for byzantine infractions.
"When I get home you better have your pants down."
The errant son withers while
waiting in a wine red leather booth
as the jukebox plays "I fell into a burning ring of fire."

I'm angry working only for tips.
I have to share them with the old sailor who
works the front counter while I serve tables.
I work much harder than he does

running back and forth
from the front counter
down the long narrow aisle
between the booths
all the way to the back door on 91st Street.
My small hands carry hot, heavy dinner specials
roast beef, mashed potatoes, green beans,
all slathered in rich brown gravy.
I resent sharing the tips.
I keep most of the money
in my waitress dress pocket
which becomes heavy
bulging at the bottom with all the coins
dirty from leaning over tables that I wipe clean.
He checks the tips can.
Disappointed
he must have known.
He never accuses me.
He just quits.
Then I get it all.

A henna-haired, weather-wrinkled old lady
runs the post-office in Strand's drug-store.
For years
every day
she comes to Wolke's Soda Parlor to eat lunch:
soup d'jour and a seeded roll.
She comes to represent everything I hate about working.
One day
I take her order
and decide not to serve her her soup and roll.
What possible purpose was served
not to serve her a bowl of soup?
She waits

not saying a word.
She waits
her old hands with red nails folded on the table
till her lunch time is up.
She leaves hungry and never comes back.
Funny
Wolke never noticed.
I guess that's what I fear most;
being there every day
and no one noticing the day I'm not there.

It happens all the time.

CIRCUMSTANCES

I am the result of an event
between my mother and my father
her contempt for him waylaid by the war.
Who had time for love or hate
when the boots were stomping closer
when the sirens were going ooo-aaa-ooo-aaa.
She would have left him after the honeymoon
but there was no place to leave him
alive in Vienna.
Buying the last steamer tickets
they boarded the Rex.
Crossing the ocean
in art deco luxury
soft velour sofas
red wine rocking gently in crystal
leaving their home
their parents
across deep waving troughs of sorrow
they step out of first class
in New York.

Yet afterwards
they had one more daughter,
an incomprehensible event
considering the circumstances of contempt.

THE HUNGER

A coyote is loose in Central Park
running down the length of Manhattan.
I don't take it too seriously.

That night
between bumpers of the taxicabs parked at curbside stands
a blue gray head with a long snout
and shaggy hair stares at pink legs passing.
It sniffs at urine from the white dog
with the rhinestone collar
as red traffic lights glint in his yellow eyes.
A hieroglyph of hunger
his dark shadow passes into Central Park.
Narrow lean feet pad up the art museum steps
pause
then wander around the back past the column
with his cartouche engraved upon it.
The dark covers his moves downtown
past the lions that have no scent
as storefronts backlight a knobby spine
bouncing on four furry bones.
Down Fifth Avenue he continues
until he sits on the sidewalk under my second floor window
where he calls to me.

Now I look down from my room above my garage in Maltby
to see him sitting on my driveway
waiting for me to feed him
my old friend, my cat.

I came to the country with a full belly
knowing only the hungers of a big city;
money, human life
couplings hidden in small rooms.

I underestimated the hunger
of the trees for the soil
of slugs for microbial waste
the hunger of cold for heat
the hunger of the wind to topple
huge trees across my lawn.
A hunger from below the stomach
from deep in the loins
pulsing.

Even in the soft golden light of an afternoon
defined by rosy clouds
a flashing shaft of lightning can open up
the jaws of Shoel
and we all fall in
head over heels over head over heels
deep into the dark throat growling
as the jaws
snap
shut.

THE GLASS

In the back of my kitchen cabinet
there's an old candle glass holding
sixty years of transparent memories.

My mother went to the temple to pray for the dead.
She never went for any other reason.
She only went to pray for the dead.
She didn't go for any joyous holidays.
She only went to pray for the dead
coming home with Grandma dressed in black
her eyes red, puffy.
She never took me to festivals
or to light candles on the Sabbath.

The only candles she lit were the Yahrzeit candles
in the glass with the arches pressed into a pattern
around the side.
At various times of the year,
two or three lights flickered and glowed in the kitchen
an altar to deathdays set up on a glass tray
on the thickly painted white wooden counter
over the drawer of old mismatched silver.
Orange flames glowed on five-year-old cheeks
staring at the glasses at night
scaring me with the shadows of dead people
moving and swaying on the kitchen ceiling
and walls behind me
reaching for me from some horrendous dark past.

After the wax had been burned away
we used the glasses to drink
Hines Black Cherry Soda
a little something sweet
to have after death.

Parachute Jump Tower at Steeplechase Park, Coney Island, N.Y

419

TEA FOR TWO

After sending her off to college
I sit on the floor in Emma's room
(which was never really Emma's room)
under white slanted walls
with maple bookcases installed
unpacking the carousels.
Cobalt blue, pink
frothy gold baroque confections
little white horses on twisted brass poles
hooves prancing
heads back, hair flying.
Musical gears grind as I wind the key:
"Tea for Two
you for me
me for you.
We will be
a happy family."

Every summer Saturday when I am nine
Daddy takes me on the subway to Coney Island.
Sun reflects off the white beach sand
smelling of rotten seaweed and dead shells.
The old wooden boardwalk
slats angled
sanded down by millions of grainy feet
splinters threatening each step.

A sea of noise
waves crashing
voices yelling, selling
honky-tonk organ music
the bang and the clang
as John Henry's hammer hits the bell.
Clacking wheels of the Cyclone's

wooden webbing above me as
screams rise and fall
slower
faster
over and over.
Saliva from the smell of burnt sugar
hot hamburger fat
french fries with hot dogs
oily Coppertone on sweat.
An odiferous stew swelling the damp sea air.
Too much to see
my child's eyes bounce around a living mosaic
of moving pieces.

But the best by far
by very far
is the carousel.
My favorite by far
by very far
is a huge moving corral of white horses.
Bedecked with jewels
square emeralds, round rubies,
bridles studded with diamonds,
their manes striped cobalt blue,
their stomping hooves golden
their tails are real horsehair
flying in the wind.
White heads tossed back they rear up
mouths grimaced open
a grotesque parody of the horses on the Parthenon
that many years later I would draw
impressed by their creamy white tones
their calm classic silky marble musculature.
But these horses are classical kitsch

candy confections with carriages framed in
golden whipped cream
good enough for Emperor Franz Joseph
("Now there was a man!" Grandma always said.)

How I love these horses.
Jumping on the wooden platform
I race for a horse on an outside ring
always the biggest and fastest.
I pull myself up and on
buckling the old leather belt
with the iron buckles and worn holes
around my waist.
A man takes my ticket
checks the belt.
I look around to see where my father stands
watching
tall, lean, gray-haired
his glasses always pointing my way.
Slowly the great carousel
heaves into its first turn
music thumping as
a large wooden drumstick with a round wooly head
mechanically strikes the side of a large vertical drum.
A Wurlitzer calliope organ launches into
"Tea for Two."
Carousel music
a melange of circus music and
early popular nineteenth century tunes
an endless river of deep vibrations.
We pick up speed.
The turning pushes me over the outside edge.
I grasp the horse's brass pole.
Greasy from the last rider's french fries

it is hard to hold onto.
My horse rising for its first jump
I can see over people heads
to where dark blue ocean and light blue sky
slowly start turning.
A starry heaven of light bulbs
glows in the tent-like ceiling
burning bubbles that rise and fall,
moving in circles until the world outside falls apart
a blur.
Colors smear
whipped behind me.
I am lost in my beautiful warm world
of color, light, motion
rising and falling.
I rush forward
music thumping
spinning sunshine
a deep state of pleasure
always to be remembered.
I lean out of the carousel hoping
to catch a gold ring between
my middle finger and thumb
as it pops out of the long metal tube
fed by a young boy.
I get the gold ring.
I always get the gold ring.
A gold ring means a free ride.
Daddy must have given the boy a dollar
"Make sure my little girl gets the gold ring."
After ten free rides
I get lightheaded
I miss the ring.
The girl behind me laughs.

I take Emma to Rye Beach
to ride the carousel and Steeplechase
to Binghamton (to ride all six)
to the Jersey shore
to Saratoga Springs.
But none of them are *that* carousel.
Yet Proustian remembrance
overwhelms me when I ride any merry-go-round
and I can
at will
enter that world of joy
filling up with emotions
that come from my child's heart,
the only inheritance from my father
paste jewels richer than real.

Fooling myself
I pretended that I bought
these little praline carousels for my daughter
but they were really for me.
Plinking "Two for Tea"
the little white horses prance
as I sit on the floor in Emma's room
(that isn't really Emma's room).

WHEN MEMORIES LAST IN THE DOORYARD BLOOMED

When I first read about
lilacs in the doorway blooming
when I was a child living in
a red brick six story apartment house in Queens
I didn't know what a lilac was.
On the the corner of Britton Avenue
was a large green bush
with huge purple flowers.
It was so beautiful
that I stared and stared
through the chain link fence
every day that I came home from PS 89.
I didn't know it was a hydrangea.

I shared a bedroom with my mother and grandmother.
Each bed had a window.
Mine had the cherry tree
which opened up a world
of pink blossoms every spring.
Kneeling on my pillow
I open the thickly painted wooden sash
then, with a jerky tug
the green dusty screen.
Leaning out I touch the pink petals
cool and fresh
smelling faintly of a life I could love.
I look at them very closely
until they are all my world.
They always turned into sour cherries.

When I see the four lilac bushes
I fulfill a literary desire to know
what a lilac is.
I bring them home to grow
in my new garden.
I kneel in the dirt.

I'm eight years old,
kneeling on the ground
in our building's backyard
digging to China with my best friend Michelle.
I'm wearing a red flowered pinafore dress
made for me by my mother.
Michelle laughs, pointing at me
"You forgot to wear underpants!"
I look and I see my bare bottom
exposed to the eyes of the Chinese.
I run home.

I dig the hole for the lilacs deeper
around old thick tree roots.
Thick pink begonias drip above my head.
Nearby with joy
I see my violets in the Matisse Pot
a blue and white striped
piece of the French Riviera
colors and forms
echoing a painting from my red period
now hanging in my living room.

I'm afraid to buy a cherry tree.
I could not stand such joy
viewing its blossoms again each spring
becoming a child again each spring
committed as I am
to be wary of tenuous happiness
tapping me on the shoulder
fleeting.

My hands pat the damp, dark soil.
Clouds move overhead
faster than crows can fly.

IF YOU LOVE ME

An advertisement is on the radio:
"Do you have thumb-sucking problems?
This is Dr. M.
I have just opened up
my new thumb-sucking clinic.
I guarantee to put an end
to this odious and destructive addiction
or your money back."
I remember the Great Thumb-Sucking War
of my childhood.

I loved sucking my thumb.
I sucked avidly
with great pleasure
until the age of four.
After all
how else does one live with someone who has lost everything
to the Great Killing Machine.
You live carefully
tiptoeing around the apartment
so that your footsteps do not wake up the dead.
The silent sounds of sucking
the pulling and relaxing of the muscles
in my cheeks
the swallowing of saliva
comforted me into silence.
My thumb was my own.
At night I would sleepwalk
with my thumb in my mouth
into the dark living room
climb into the blue wing chair
that sat in front of the turned off TV
and watch grainy black and white Farmer Gray cartoons
in my dreams.

My mother became desperate.
Afraid that I would enter public school
buck-toothed and labeled "slow" she resolved
to end my "odious and destructive" habit.

Mother tried everything.
She rubbed capsicum powder on my thumb.
My lips burned but I licked it off
then sucked my thumb.
She coated it with bitter alcohol.
I licked it off then sucked my thumb.
She painted nail polish on
she wrapped it in scotch tape.
I overcame all obstacles.
She threatened to cut my thumb off.
I held onto to it
it was mine.
She and I fought over
this part of my body
I as determined as any child could be
to keep control of it
she as determined as any mother
to claim it as her own.

Then one day she challenged me:
"If you love me,
you'll stop sucking your thumb."
Defiance gave way to fear.
I knew I had to prove to her that I loved her
by giving up my little life's greatest pleasure.
Afraid that I would be thrown out of my bed
my kitchen
her life
the way she had thrown Daddy out of her life

I had no doubt that she could
and would do it.
I stopped sucking my thumb.

In her victory she hugged me
she loved me
she let me live with her.
The emotional aftershocks lasted
down the years.

I became afraid of men's thumbs.
I knew they had a hidden power over me.
I would become addicted again
to a joy that was not permitted.
How many times did I leave a room
to enter the darkness of night
with only dreams to sustain me
a limp thumb left behind.

As long as she was alive
I didn't have a child.
It was the only thing
she couldn't control.
She had taken my thumb away once
now she would have no pleasure of the
thumb I had married.
Soon after she died I had Emma.
I was by then forty-three.

Yet it's never over.
In my deepest dreams
I still watch grainy black and white cartoons
in which a gigantic thumb runs
around the barn yard
chasing a frightened little girl.

OLD MAN MEDITATION

First his nose falls off
huge granite chunks
bouncing off the ground
as they fall across the sky
over the evergreen trees
crushing rabbits and deer
powdering the gray gravel
strewn down the mountainside.
Then the steel cables snap
that had held his cheeks in place
for insignificant centuries
as the iron petons
driven in to support his head
drop.
The skull falls to pieces
a new Ozymandias for our time.
Craggy gray boulders
lie strewn across the landscape.
No one saw it happen
or felt the reverberations in the earth.
People stand around at the base of the mountain
looking up
mourning their Old Man.

I am a mountain
sitting on a wide strong base
rising to the sky.
Sit straight.
I am forever.
I sit.
I sit.
My face falls apart.

GNARLED ROOTS

I have a small ivory leather album with a gold buckle
the words Graduation, Autographs, Peggy, PS 89
engraved in tarnished green gold.
In it my grandmother wrote a German poem for me
an elegant rhyme in three quarter time.

Under a white goose down comforter
her gray hair on soft white pillows
the reading lamp creating dark shadows under her chin
she recited from memory
Shiller and Goethe
romantics in pain that would stalk my artistic life forever.
Children died
poets cried desires denied
black forest branches wet with rain
slashed at my face while stumbling on the path
to a high craggy cliff.
Raising my fist
I railed at a still pagan god and the elements.
This was the poetic food of my childhood
the warm crumbs of words still on my chin.

In sixth grade Miss Denman
made me memorize poetry.
Selecting works from
Louis Untermeyer's anthology she
drove into my brain iron spikes that
to this day would show up on an x-ray.
"Ulalee, Ulalee" I cried while
"The highwayman came
riding, riding, riding."
Something there was that didn't love a wall.
This was not the poetry of Baudelaire,

Eliot or either Dylan.
This was the poetry of childhood
that gave us hope;
the belief that we could understand art.
The existential pain came later.

"ON YOUR LEFT!"

My legs pump gently
in the late afternoon
blue reflections
of trees in water.

"On your left!"
A black butt streaking past me
calves bare bulging biceps.
Fifty-one years since I last rode a bicycle.
Memories of streets lost to malls.
Fairyland.
Kissena Park.
Down Corona Avenue
buried trolley rails shining through the asphalt
on their curving way over
the orange pebbled concrete of Newtown Bridge.
Howard Johnson's peaked orange roof.
Intense thoughts of a fifteen-year-old on a Rudge.

"On your left!"
I saw it in a thrift shop
all French and silver.
It was 35 years old.
I guess I bought it to prove
that it could still work.
Just like me.
I sit upright
and carefully
a woman past a certain age
a red Pierre Deux handbag tied to the handlebars
(with my Blue Cross card inside, just in case).
Wearing a light blue roller blade helmet in
anticipation of World War One.

"On your left!"
My wobble is dangerous to your health.
You fear me.

Where are you going
passing me so fast, so intense?
Life is to be savored,
like a really good cappuccino.
He flashes by.
When you get there
you're there
you turn around
and you're here.
I ride on alone
the wheels turn alone.
A good way to get away.

"On your left!"
I pass fifty gray waterfront "homes to lease"
ticky tacky little boxes all in a row.
A lady with a cat on her lap smiles at me.
A Blackberry in the sun.
Cow smell, horse smell
great hit, cheering crowd.
Empty green benches.
I remember the windmills of Holland thirty years
ago
tall tree shadows in the slanting sun.
My crotch starts to burn.
I didn't know it could still burn.
It's been a long time.
Joggers panting in Hindi.
Under the overpass.
Up is hard
very hard.
I struggle to stay in motion every day.

I shout
"On your left!"

I peddle faster!
I am running with the wolves.
I am going for the old gold
with silver threads amongst.

OMPHALOS

Delphi was where I first saw the Omphalos.
It glowed in the warm light
an egg shaped reddish stone
high as half a man.
Here
without doubt
was the knobby navel of the world
the center of it all.

In the black and white photograph
(by an unknown photographer)
I walk alone through the ruins of Delphi.
I paid a few drachma for it.
An olive tanned sixteen-year-old almost woman
in a flowered dress with thin straps
shoulders bare and shiny.
On my own Grecian "Odyssey"
island to island
over the cobalt waters
I've come to this sacred place alone.
The oracle laughs with joy
at this virgin's love of
beauty is truth,
truth beauty.
Oracular fumes from stone labia
predict a life of sacrifice to the goddess.

The scrubby mountains
enclose temple walls
felled by earthquakes
the tantrums of
an ignored goddess
looking for attention.
Now she lies all over the ground

her body scattered
as curious onlookers poke at her sacred places.

I travel alone
without my mother.
Disappointed I was born a girl
my mother refused to give me a name.
After three days the nurse nagged
"You're going home today.
You have to name the baby.
Name the baby.
Name the baby."

I put two fingers
on my navel
my own omphalos.
Pushing in
I feel the aching presence of her,
pulsing.
The unwanted beginnings of my
life are still here.
I know it.
I know it as well as
I know the rain
that runs down the face of a child crying
when it is not picked up.

THE THRIFT STORE

"No, you can't have it Ron."
"But it's solid brass. At least three pounds."
"It's too ugly."
"It" is a four-inches-long by three-inches-high
  brass rabbit that's been made into a stapler.
"It's only $3.99. That's really cheap for all that brass."
"If it was solid gold, OK,
  but I don't need a big brass rabbit stapler in the house.
  That's final."
"You're very unreasonable."

My daughter and her boyfriend
wander the aisles searching for old clothes
the only acceptable attire in Portland
which they tear apart, cut, resew.
I think it's admirable;
except for the shoes.

Once, in an outdoor flea market in Manhattan
a big hubbub arose in a corner.
The word spread quickly;
"Parker died! He died in his booth. Parker's dead."
In minutes
like the old women in Zorba the Greek
the booth was stripped clean.
After the ambulance left
Ron picked up a worn library stool
lying tilted over on the asphalt.
We took it home
where it still remains
a memorial to every old Mr. Parker.

And so Ron and I spend our older years
recycling our dishes and our fears.

I recycle my memories of life in New York
into poems
hoping they will someday
be of interest to someone else
who picks up my book in a thrift store.

THE ROBE

Unpacking a carton labeled "memorabilia"
I find a child's bathrobe with the label
"Laddie Robes"
my mother's brand
folded by my father in my mother's factory.

Standing at the plywood table
he lays the robe on its back
pins the front closed
pinches the top and bottom with
each hand and flips it over.
Shoulders and sleeves are folded into the back
belt inserted, smoothed
it is tagged and put on the pile
to be sent to the buyer, a Mr. Green.
By some miracle this one has escaped loss
the only remaining robe
a sacred shroud.

My mother was a seamstress
with a Certificate from the
"Lehranstalten fur Kleidermachen"
in Vienna, dated March 20, 1929.
Arriving in New York in 1939
she first worked at Saks Fifth Ave. on her knees
hemming wealthy flatulently affluent ladies
thin as only the rich can afford to be
smoking Tarrytons
standing on a carpeted platform;
three mirrors
three reflections of a black evening dress
cut on the bias
slim and silky.
Pins in her mouth

she can smell her crotch
as she bends down to adjust the hem.

Years later she opens her own sewing factory.
I'm a three-year-old child
sitting in thick gray lint
under a large plywood table
playing with zippers in narrow cardboard boxes.
Six-inch zippers with silver teeth.
Ten-inch zippers with flashing gold teeth.
I see my father's feet
gray trousers
his cuffs full of short threads
as he stands at the table folding robes.
Industrial sewing machines roar like lions
the steam presser hisses
pipes hot
threatening to burst any moment
like my mother's temper.
The elevated number seven IRT train screetches outside.
I wander in canyons of leaning cartons
tied with jute twine.
I watch the flowered, dotted, striped
curved backs and bare arms
of women sitting
sewing.
Under the machines their feet on steel platforms:
toes up heels down
heels up toes down.
Smelling of machine oil and sweat
they call me "bambino."
They smile at me with flashing gold teeth.
Years later
Hungarians making horsehair petticoats

give me ten cent tips for getting them cold soda.
They smile at me with flashing gold teeth.
Years later
Colombians offer me deep black coffee.
They smile at me with flashing gold teeth.

She cries when the union forces her to close her factory.
Cheaply bought
the Chinese buyers carry out her sewing machines:
the double needle
the merrow
the button-hole maker.
They leave the steam presser.
As the truck hauls it all away,
she stands
on the sidewalk alone
her feet surrounded by
sharp black and white shadows
from the sun beaming through
the train tracks above.

I walk into that grungy storefront
hers for so many years
cracked walls
plaster pealing
tin ceiling leaking rotten wood dust
the floor patched with metal squares.
In the backyard I find that small patch of soil
where my father once grew four tomato plants
as my mother laughed at him.
Humming fans from the clothing cleaners
on the other side of the alley
still blow out moist hot air smelling of solvents.
The lint

still under the plywood table
is undisturbed.
Dusty, tattered boxes of zippers
their corroded gold teeth no longer usable
sit lost in dark corners.

I sit here in Maltby
that beautifully folded Laddie robe on my lap
in my spotless white studio
that has no zippers or lint.
I wish for a child to play
under the table at my feet.

THE WHISTLER

It's dark and damp in the country tonight.
Muffled bird sounds come over the fence.
Dogs and sirens howl from afar
as they tear down Maltby Road.
Grass rustles in frog throats.
No one whistles around here.

We called him simply "The Whistler."
Lying in my white feather bed at night
in the ground floor corner apartment in Queens
my mother and grandmother in opposite
dark corners of the silent room
street lamp stripes diagonal on the wall
I could hear him approach from the corner
of Elmhurst Avenue
at eleven-fifteen each night.
Soulfully whistled
his tune grew louder and louder
until it passed beneath my
open at the top window.
Minor keyed Doppler tones touched
the far shadows
of the block.
As he went on his mysterious way
his clear notes floated behind on the air.
What he looked like
where he went
I never knew.

It rained dark puddles last night.
I thought I heard the balloon man whistling
but he doesn't whistle anymore
not since I was wee.

LOUIE'S FRANGIPANI

Late one night,
the heavy fragrance of frangipani fills my house.
Wafting on the darkness
the scent grows stronger as I enter my living room.
The full moon shines through the windows
as my bare feet glide over white light and
blue shadows on the wood floor.
The plant in the corner is ululating waves of jasmine.
My dracaena cane
the nine-foot-long green snake
that has stood in the corner of my life
for forty-seven years
has bloomed for the first time.

Calling for a lover under a
false tropical moon in the furnace warmth
its white flowers exude a clear sticky fluid
that drips on long green leaves
dropping to the floor
to dry as small sticky crystals.
Alas, there are no bees or butterflies
allowed in my convent of the night.
It remains alone.

Ron bought my Dracaena Massangeana in 1961
for three dollars from the back of Louie's Plant Truck
on the corner of Sixth Avenue and Twenty Fourth Street.
Living in dark corners over the years it survived,
growing longer and more gangly.
In 2006, in a huge Holman's Moving Truck
it shook its way to Seattle in a damp black plastic bag.
It was placed in the corner (again) of my living room
this time by a window
where I look at it now in astonishment

inhaling its perfume.

I wish I knew what woke it from its long sleep.
If this dracaena cane can bloom again in its old age,
why can't I?

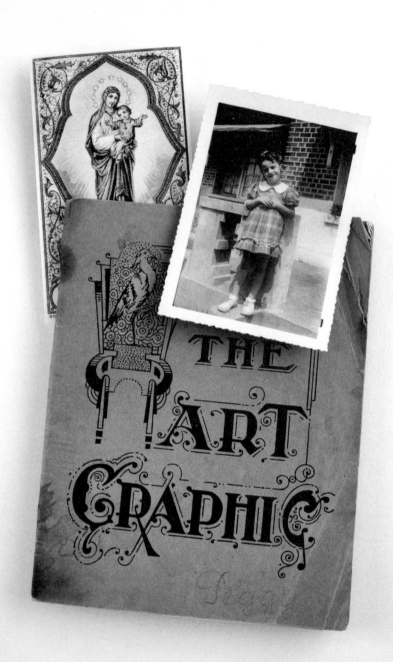

THE LADY IN BLUE

Yesterday I framed my Fra Angelico prints of angels.
I had bought them many years ago in Florence.
Set into a long gold frame with
four little squares edged in gold rope
the winged musician angels float in a gold sky
harps, violas, trumpets held high.

The lady in the blue dress is beautiful.
Her robe
the blue of the deepest blue sky day,
swirls around her feet.
Covering her golden hair is a blue gauze veil,
her blue eyes gaze upward,
her eyebrows a pencil thin line,
barely there.
A tiny red mouth between pale peach cheeks
in an oval face tilted slightly to the right.
She floats on a cloud,
sun rays streaming from behind her gold haloed head.
Golden stars surround her.
She holds a little golden haired child
that gazes at me.
A gilded frame of lilies in green leaves
winds around the edge of the card,
the size of a playing card,
given to me by Soeur Ann Marie,
the nun who is my teacher.

It is a painting of the Virgin Mary
but I don't know that.
I am the little five-year-old
Jewish girl in the jungle
with no other school to go to
than the local Catholic Convent school.

My sister takes me every morning
on the back of her bicycle.
When it rains
great big drops one by one spaced far apart
turn the road to mud
so we walk instead.
I love the picture of the Lady in Blue.
She is so beautiful.
But my mother takes it away
after she finds out that I have been to confession
on my knees at the altar
had opened my lips for the wafer-of-no-taste
to melt on my tongue
had sipped sweet wine from the small silver chalice.
After that I sit in the back of the church
the outcast alone in the dark
denied the warm light of the candles
the ancient smell of frankincense and myrrh.

The language is French,
and thrown on my own devices
I struggle the best I can in kindergarten.
A sheet is hung between two poles and
Voila! a puppet theater.
Our shoes are the puppets.
One by one the children
duck behind the sheet
put the shoes on their hands
hold them high up for all to see
and make them talk and sing:
"Ainsi font, font, font,
les petites marionnettes."
The nun never calls on me to sing.

I still have the little paper notebook,
the words "The Art Graphic" printed
elegantly on its now brittle brown cover.
I still see it on the wooden desk
I shared with a little boy who once peed in the classroom
a wet puddle spreading under us.
Sister was very angry.
Inside the book is my artwork;
a sailboat made of folded pink paper with a French flag
a sitting black cat torn from shiny black paper
two camels and a palm tree colored brown and green.
The word "Noel" with a candle.
Childish icons from a lost French civilization in the Congo.
How strange then, that my mother chose to pack it
and bring it back with her to New York
so I could now re-find it in Maltby.

To this day I love images of angels
blue veils with stars and halos
feathery wings on their shoulders.
They are the messengers.
I see them climbing the ladders between heaven and earth
their toes barely touching the rungs
as they rise upwards.
I see myself with wings.
I fly up into a golden sky
stars floating all around me
singing.

THE BOWERY

When I turn nineteen
I move into Ron's loft on the Bowery
deep in New York's Lower East Side.
We sleep late
quietly inhaling the smoky sweet smell of burning glazes
that waft up through the wide floorboards
from the hot pottery kilns downstairs.
William Wasserman,
our landlord on Bond Street
manufactures thick white cheap plates
with green stripes around the edge
all used by the Chinese restaurants we love to eat in.
For eighty dollars a month
we ignore the brain damage being done to us
by the vapor of his labors.
A small loft with frosted blue north light
the tin ceiling leaks
tiny wood splinters onto our bedsheets.
We live in an earlier world of New York in the 1860's.
I wake up on the inside of the bed
against the cool rough wall
afraid to sleep on the outside
ever since I saw "The Hands of Orloff."
My easel is a cross in the corner.
I have talent.
My bitter old man painting teacher yells at me
"Stay home and have babies!"
I raise ferns in the shadows.
The earthy smell of loam
covers the dank smell of a hundred years of use.
I'm on my own now.
Trucks rumble on slippery cobblestones outside
shiny with the shushing rain.
that once washed away the horse manure.
One spring afternoon I was sitting on a bench
in Washington Square when
a pickpocket snatched a wallet.

A policeman mounted on a chestnut colored horse just happened to be there.
He began chasing the thief.
Now this was the last thing the robber expected
to be chased down the cobblestone streets of
Greenwich Village by a policeman on a horse.
He ran
legs pumping hard
twisting around in fear to look.
The horse was fast, agile
gaining on him.
I watched them as they streaked down Bond Street.
It was a wonderful sight to see
as they raced past me from one century into another.

THE WAGES OF SIN

My childhood bathroom had
peach tiled walls around
a peach colored tub.
Soft edges of thick peach paint
stuck the window shut
as tan nylons hung drying on wooden spokes on the wall.

I scream at Mama:
"I hate you, I hate you!"
as I run into the bathroom
where I sit on the toilet
sobbing
a six-year-old
with cramps of
frustration and fear.
My mother opens the door
and stands in front of me
her stomach thin and flowered.
"You see, God is punishing you for hating me"
she says
hands on hips.
I cry and cry
my chest shaking.
Suddenly I retch
and throw up
into the peach tub.
No control
crying and retching
I can't stop.
"There, now the evil is coming out of you."
Soothing my forhead my mother croons
"You won't hate me anymore.
You'll be good now."
Now I know what evil looks like
orange stinky smelling lumps
that are coming from inside me.
I'm terrified as the demon leaves me.
My exorcism complete

I whimper my sobs:
"I'll be good Mama."

I grow up into a bulemic adult,
throwing up my evil
a confession
whenever there is a deviation from goodness.
Mollifying mother keeps me from obesity.
I became an artist.
It was either create
or throw up.
The force of emotions constantly erupting
like magma from the deep earth
hardening as it flowed inside me
hardened me.

When I leave home,
my artwork is thrown out by my mother
put into the incinerator to burn.
Ashes in the air
it falls to the ground
blackening the window sills
on our block.

I loved taking a bath with my mother.
Sheltered with her arms around me
the warmth was everything
that I needed to protect me.
But that was before the fall.
That was before I ate of the fruit
of defiance.
That was before I threw up into the tub.

I'VE NEVER SEEN A MADRONE TREE

A flock of birds flying together
landing in this town or the other
joining
separating
a black ribbon fluttering on the blue air,
their calls softly sung or loudly croaked
recognized by one another.
The one or two lone hawks are
committed to not eating the more fragile-boned.

They fly in the orange sunset
landing on a madrone tree
or the roof of a crumbling arroyo house
on the side of the hot dusty road
a chicken running through one's feet
ready to be plucked
then dipped into bitter chocolate
for a few US dollars.

They fly over rock dark beaches
wild sucking waves
with dark fearsome shapes hunching
through the surface of the Pacific.
Bright hot heat of rocks
slowly turns into wet damp moss
as the river of words winds northward
always the orange setting sun beside them.

There are few thunderstorms here—
the ear shattering kind that breaks your bones
just the wind
a fearful wind
and the fire that consumes.
Faces here

turn to the lowering orb every evening
speaking words of finality and Zen emptiness
the daily quenching of fire by water.
Poets walk into the waves
towards the round gold light
with their hands held before them
fingers disappearing
leaving green spots behind.

Where I was born I could see
the sun rise blue and cool every morning
across the black silver edged line of the Atlantic.
And the birds flew so fast
I hardly heard them call
but I saw them flying down the canyon walls of steel
across the hot asphalt
as the orange setting bouncing ball of a sun set
squeezed between two hard black skyscrapers
like a heart beating in a breathless chest.
Words fell out of windows
to be carried on the black backs of ravens
landing on trembling sunflowers.

The endlessly unrelenting every day dawn
began the hard sidewalk pounding
work of words,
old years firing up kilns across rusty iron bridges
down to where the dead suck sugared limes
north to where granite faced poets
fall off mountains
crushing cool sweet smelling balsams.

Of a summer evening
on a soft warm white sanded beach

a blue chill wind blows dark clouds
that shadow us.
Sadly packing our blankets
painfully donning sandpaper shoes
we run home before the dark falls down.

I stand on the shore
cold salty waves lapping at my feet
both there
and here.

DAY FOR NIGHT

I've been woken up by
the beaming light of a full moon in my face.
I slide silently to the living room.
Blue light,
white edged
trees cast long sharp shadows
on the silver lawn.
This is a different full moon
from the dusky yellow pumpkin moon
low on the Adirondack monadnocks
thrown up into the northern sky.
I have woken up one hundred years later
with the hairs of
an old lady kind of beard.
I lift up my full face to look and
the light smooths out my wrinkles
my skin glows blue in a mirror.
It is "Day for Night" light.

We are watching Francoise Truffaut's
film "Day for Night."
To turn daylight into nightlight
in black and white film
he uses a very deep blue filter.
Ron and I are in the old St. Mark's Cinema
on Second Avenue
fondly nick-named "the Itch"
We never sit in the front row
reserved for the Hell's Angels
who swagger in
beered up and bearded
to sit on their spines.
We
the hoi-polloi of New York's Lower East Side

of the 1960's
sit in rows of stoned silence
eating Alice B.'s brownies
flickering moon faces
all turned toward the light.
We stare for six hours at
"Eraserhead," "Freaks," and "El Poto."
We breathe in Carne's "Les Enfants du Paradis."
as this romantic memory of 1840 Paris
unreels the tale of the great mime Deburau.
Frenchmen in black frock coats and tall narrow top hats
women with long white necks
in great thick dresses like swinging silk bells,
live in small wooden rooms.
Deburau is the original Pierrot clown
with the black capped white face
small red painted lips
always laughing, frightened, sly
crying.
We turn our daylights into nights.
We turn ourselves into dark loving glow worms,
flickering fire flies.
Afterwards
near dawn
we stagger out
into the night turning to day
to go eat cabbage soup at The Kiev.

I know Deburau well.
He is the small white faced Pierrot doll
in a harlequin suit with
the tear at the corner of his eye.
I am three years old and
my family is doing piecework around the kitchen table.

We are feeding ourselves by
cutting, sewing and stuffing
little cloth clown dolls.
Each large white plastic face
has a star shaped tear
falling from the corner of his outer eye.
The faces arrive inside out
like the man in the moon on the wrong side.
It is my job to pop the faces
right side out.
My little hands grab both edges
snap them over then
I put them on the table.
Grandma is sewing the seams for the body
made of one purple piece of
cheap shiny harlequin rayon with
a yellow diamond pattern.
Daddy uses an old wooden cooking spoon
to stuff them with lambs wool.
We sit in a circle
no fighting
too scared for arguments.
Eating comes first
then the rent
I can't tell you how many we made
because I was too young to count.

At the age of thirteen in Carnegie Hall
I watch the great French mime
Marcel Marceau move across life's stage.
A harlequin in black tights
a soft river of emotions
a red rose in his hand
he breaks my heart.

Speechless silence so deep
primordial fears and love so vast
that we return to that childish age
before we learn words to express what we feel.
If I could rid myself of words
I'd be a better poet.

Years later
in a blue painting period of my own
I study Picasso's harlequin clowns.
Blue *veniss cereuses* faces
thin and haggard
haunting white smokey air
tired pain in their bones.
I understand their long thin thighs
covered in purple with pale yellow diamond patterns.
I mix endless shades of blue to evoke
the colorless underworld of
a place that I now inhabit with
harlequins long lost in absinthe.
My paintbox smells like the old lineseed oil
in reused backdrops made of old tent canvas
the long cheap bristle stained brushes
are worn down from scrubbing.
Sad eyes with long thin fingers look
toward me
then away from me.
I work alone.
As an artist I will always work alone.

The moon has moved to the front of the house.
In the night for day light shadows point at me.
I wipe a shining star from the corner of my eye
and go back to bed.

A MAYFLY BLOW

It's a clear night in the Cattaraugus Mountains of western
New York State as we drive back to our motel.
Our headlights show a two lane country road
as it winds through the dark.

We have just left Rock City
one of those little-known sites of prehistoric worship
hidden in these mountains.
I wandered through rock openings
in three-story-high black quartz boulders
walked deep down on fossilized ocean floor streets,
crunching calcium shells
my shoulders scraping glossy smooth tall walls
darkly brooding
cold to the touch.
I look up at a sliver of blue feeling an ancient presence.
Some places keep their old gods.

The night is cooler so we wind the windows up.
Around a curve
we hear the *shuss* of water.
Over a low bridge and
suddenly our headlights disappear.
The windshield goes black.
I can't see.
I turn on the windshield wipers.
Black blood smears the glass.
Windshield fluid makes streams of wings, bodies
rivulets of mass destruction.
The side windows disappear too as I drive on slowly
peering through moving holes of vision.

In town at the car wash,
under the blue fluorescent lights
millions of crushed insects bleed,
wings flickering on green metal.
I feel queasy.

We don't even know what they are.
An old guy walks up;
"Looks like you drove into a mayfly blow.
They all mate over the river this time of year."
He walks away into the dark.
It takes us hours to clean off all the squashed mayflies.
We just keep buying three minutes more of hot sudsy water.
They're in the grill
in door cracks
crusting our plastic Big Mac storage bin on the roof.
All I keep thinking is
"thank God we had the windows up."

That's how life happens.
Without warning a huge mass flies at you out of nowhere
instantly blinding you with its darkness.
Understanding it is impossible at the time.
Only later, after surveying the damage
to your heart
to your ego
to your naïve expectations
can an explanation be found.
I've been through many a mayfly blow in my life.
They've left me wary of crossing those small bridges
to somewhere else.

ROCK OF AGES

Now at home
I sit at my front window in my rocking chair
sipping my hot cappuccino slowly.
Two huge black crows
fly across the top of my cup
as my mind flies through memories
of the cloak wrapped goat man in the dunes.
I drag my feet up orange rocky hills
bare and dusty
biting unripe olives
in a piercing white light from everywhere.
Dust blows from the south
turning the dead turquoise sea to a misty blur.
My footprints don't remember
having walked this way before.
I was here and then I wasn't.
Time was once full
now it's empty.
Ululating voices sigh
as fingers sift sand and pebbles.
Sharp shadows cut my feet.

I walk up the slanting ramps of a ziggurat
on which the prophets trudge
up and down
praying in low songs.
Dark black etched shadows of Abraham and Isaac
climb slowly on the scratched rock.
How do I begin
when the fear of not finishing
extends its fistful of dirt to thud on my coffin.
I have come here and found arrows falling from the sky.
Here's a smooth round yellow stone in your palm
for when I die.

These are the golden rocks that rained
upon the cities of the plain.
These are the rocks that fell on me.
I find them once again.

"You killed Christ!"
the three Irish boys scream at us
lips pinched
blue eyes glaring:
"Let's stone them!"
We are two nine-year-olds trapped in the alley
by tribal wolves from PS 89.
These three judges
standing on piles of bricks from a
demolished Queens tenement
protected by a chain link fence
obeying scripture
vigorously and biblically
throw bricks at the two harlots.
We flatten into the building wall
backs against the hardness
trying to disappear
to take shelter from this rain of stones.
Sharp pains in my shoulders
my thighs and chest
my side as I turn my face away.
I crouch in the corner
covering my head.
Like Lot's wife I look back
see a piercing white light
then blood runs through my eyes
down my face.
I wail
a wail so fierce

and so high
that the three judges turn to stone
then run.
A white wet towel falls from a window
to land at my feet.
I run home to Dr. Brodie's office.
Running through his waiting room
full of chicken pox, mumps, measles, polio
I arrive bloodied,
alone.
Stitching up my face he asks "Why?"
"Because I killed Christ."
My anger smolders.
A year later another Irish kid
corners me in my backyard.
Again I hear the words
"You killed Christ."
Rage:
a train coming out of a black tunnel
emerges from my chest.
I attack
pushing him to the ground
and I grab his head with both hands
and smash it again and again into the sidewalk
until he has a halo of blood.
I run home.
After dinner the doorbell rings.
With my mother I go to the door.
She opens it inward.
There is Michael with his mother:
"Look what your daughter did to my son!"
"My daughter? She's just a little girl."
"Tell your daughter to stay away from my son."
Mother closed the door

looked at me and said
"Well done."
For sixty years I've wandered
sixty hundred just as well.
All my footsteps are the same
all the same the tales I tell.
The rocks of old are buried
but the bones will rise again,
children huddle under covers as the towers fall on them.
Rocks and stones and pebbles
flow down wadis to the sea
as I slide into in the shadows
as I try to bend the knee.
Truth is burning hot here
black smoke rising to the skies,
for the towers still are falling
lying there before my eyes.

I'm climbing steps with aching bones
I yearn for home
to which I will carry rocks—
selected for color and shape
plucked out of the desert
then deposited into a wooden box
as souvenirs.
One day I will look at them and say
"Where did all these rocks come from?"
and throw them out.

*Written February 2009 upon my return from
visiting Israel during the Gaza war.*

POTHOLES

My car bounces into the many huge potholes
in the gravel road down our street.
The wheel and my head jerk back and forth.
These holes are getting bigger and more numerous.
They are in front of the wooden house
of the man who's supposed to fill them.
He just put his wife into a deeper hole.
He believes she will rise again.
All I want is for these miserable potholes to be filled.
I'm not asking for a miracle.

AFTER THE BALL IS OVER

After the ball is over,
After the break of morn,
After the dancers' leaving,
After the stars are gone;
Many a heart is aching,
If you could read them all;
Many the hopes that have vanished,
After the ball.

          — "After the Ball," 1890's popular song

The Good Times Band is playing
on the stage of the Senior Center ballroom.
Sparse gray hair, blue suits, old sax
they gently play "Tennessee Waltz"
as the woman glides in her wheelchair
her pusher sliding her feet in three-quarter time.
The smooth gym floor is perfect for dancing on Wednesdays;
silver memories suspended in time.

Two gentlemen are sitting on either side of me
breathing heavily after dancing
gnarled hands on knees
smooth bottomed shoes
striped shirt bellies curved over western belt buckles.

She's in her eighties in a blue spangled sweater
shiny black pumps with straps
silver hair in a beehive
still a hoofer and very
picky about her partners.

The band picks it up with "Sweet Georgia Brown"
in a quick two-step.
Feet in reflections move faster in small circles.

"Everybody's doin' it, doin' it, doin' what?"
Everybody's doing it, the Turkey Trot."

Chests heaving
hips hurting
after an hour the crowd thins
leaving the floor to the more hearty.

The slim, younger couple in their fifties
enjoy the afternoon.
Accomplished dancers—
he leads her backwards
palm tight against the small of her straight back—
she in her little black dress
calves like closed fists.

I admire the brave ones,
women blind to the ravages of age
not afraid
like me
to say "yes" to an older, older man.
"What could possibly happen now, mother?"
Coat hangers put away
the old Molly Blooms of the ballroom
"Yes," they say, "yes, yes."
There are still those of us who sit
in chairs on the side and watch.
I put my head down
remembering.

I'm thirteen in the huge gym for
my Junior High School Graduation Prom
the awful band playing "Blue Suede Shoes."
I stand with excess crinolines sticking out

a corsage on my pointy left breast.
No one asks me to dance.
We rejects stand with our arms crossed over our chests
weight on one leg
other knee bent.
I turn my back on a blond slow dancing girl.

Later, I look across the room
and see her resting on the floor,
her back against the pale green tile wall
her frilly skirt hiked up on her bent knees.
A red stain is showing on her white underwear.
How am I to deal with this painful vision?
Tell her
and end what
is available for all to see
with death by embarrassment.
Not tell her
and continue the exhibition
of her womanly shame.
Eyes quickly look and flick away.
Boys have now parked themselves
to see and snigger
grins among the pimples.

I move to her
bend down my face to her face
telling her
watching her eyes widen in horror.
Her legs snap down.
I walk away.

Later
on my way to the bathroom

I see her in the hallway
face to the tile wall
crying on her fists.
But what can I say?
I have said enough.
So I leave the dance
walking the long walk home alone
in the humid darkening night
my new white flats scraping the sidewalk.

And the band plays on with
"Dancing Cheek to Cheek"
as I watch Fred and Ginger dip and sway
feet tripping to the fox-trot
pacemakers working overtime.

THE OLD MARE

On a warm Sunday morning in May
I walk by the silver haired horse
and stop to share the day.
She munches the grass
with a low grinding sound
takes a half step forward
now and then,
here and there.
No longer frisky
she is further calmed
by the tranquilizer pellets
that her owner
now not so young herself anymore
and a little dotey
feeds her to keep
from having to deal with her moody needs.
I look into her wet dark eyes
and see my future.

It's a blustery Sunday morning in October.
The silver haired mare has disappeared
sometime between May and October.
The swaying brown grass in the field is knee high
with no horse to pull and chomp.
Her old owner
bending over
still in her tan riding pants
weeds the front lawn alone.
They were friends for thirty years.
The blue tarp covering something over there
flaps,
flaps in the wind.
Looks like they're going to sell the house.

HER SILENCE

It is autumn
a time of dying and becoming cold.
Driving down Maltby Road
red and gold
leaves race toward me at warp speed.
The radio is off
windows closed
car inside silent.
I clear my throat
the sound startling me.
I drive on turning north.
I know that there are
so many miles between us
so many white dashes on the asphalt.
We are
by now
twenty-eight years apart.

I see you small
far away
as if looking through the wrong end of a telescope.
I see your dying face still alive
pale skin taut
silent as a stone
blue eyes staring at the foot of the bed.
You don't look at me
never see me
as if I wasn't there
as if I had died before you.
Your mouth tightly shut
unsmiling
hard edged
never spoke again to me.
No sad good-bye smile for the invisible ghost unseen

always siting by your side waiting.
Waiting for something other than the anger.

You left tight jawed
relentlessly unforgiving
my inability to save you.
I was born to help you.
I was here all those years
to make you laugh.
Now I'm helpless.
Forgive me.
You loved me once.
I could see it in your eyes then.
Is it too much to ask,
for you to
say "I love you" before you go.

For four months I flit
around you
like a glass moth
looking for some warmth
a glimmer of light from your pale eyes staring.
I bang my heart against the silence
until it shatters.
Shards of love
are swept under the bed
crunching underfoot when I go home each night
defeated
alone.

I sit for months
next to a mother that died
forty years before in those other flames.

Gray ashes in the white bed.

COLOSSUS

The New York night is dark, quiet.
The statue stands alone in the harbor facing east
her robe's folds billowing out behind her
gold torchlight flickering light on the choppy waves.
Small fluorescent green squares glow in an arc.
The rising sun of a new dawn shines seductively on her face.
The massive green sandaled foot moves.
It steps off the pedestal
toes huge and clutching the ground
a sound that reverberates through the air
shaking distant skyscrapers.
The second foot follows with a clanging clump
as she steps off the island onto the water.

Trailing a cast iron staircase
holding her torch forward
she begins to stride across the harbor
towards the ever growing day.
Ducking under the Verrazano Narrows Bridge
she moves toward Europe.
Waves washing the bottom of her skirts
she strides,
huge steps,
hurrying to her destiny.
She passes France
striding quickly over the land of her birth
huge iron feet pounding Hungary and Bulgaria
to Greece—
where she stops and looks around at the ruins of her life.

Now barefoot she steps over the Mediterranean
her heel shaking Rhodes where the Colossus
forged from cannons and swords

to welcome strangers to a safe harbor
was melted and reforged into cannons and swords again.

Her footsteps shake the solid rocks of pharoahs
buried in square cut tombs
forever the lords of their domains.
Heavy long strides leave behind silent green tears
to fall on the cracked domes of Constantinople.

She cries out when her feet are cut on Syrian rocks
leaving sunken bloody footprints to dry in the bright sun.
She runs
green skirts flying
hair ragged
torch burning lower
fuel dying
further south to Africa
where they catch her.

The liberated make her kneel down at a guillotine
inherited from France.
There they cut her head off.
It rolls down,
down into the desert
landing on its cheek
in the Valley of the African Rift
her crown's thorns pointing to the sky
sad eyes staring
ragged bronze neck hacked open.
The yellow sand blows over her green face
slowly burying her.
"Look on my works ye mighty and despair."

THE DAY WE BURIED HARRY
(A TRUE OPERA IN THREE ACTS)

"Mr. Barnett? He dead."

Act 1: Death

"Don't spend no money on a funeral"
Harry ordered.
"Just cremate me."
Cremate him?
Jews don't get cremated.
Not since World War Two anyway.
"Bury me with my sister Elenore."
"Where is Elenore?," I ask.
"I already put her ashes in our mother's grave.
I want to be with the two of them."

The day before the final breaths,
  as he lay there making strange grunting sounds
I said to him:
"Harry, when you get there
  take care of Emma.
Watch over her from there
  you hear me?"
He grunted assent.
He knew what to do.
He believed in life after death.

Abandoned by Louis
the classical violinist father
with a wife and family in
Cincinatti
Chicago
New York
and Boston,
Harry was dedicated to having Ron

Louis's grandson
learn the violin.
Until the violin teacher played with Ron's ass.
That ended that with a baseball bat.
Harry's mother was a cook in a Boston hotel
until she became paralyzed
and could no longer stir.
Put into a Catholic orphanage
he was raised by ruler whacking
palm slapping nuns
as he climbed across the wooden table
for the last hot potato to warm his cold fingers.

He believed in Hell
his mind a confused place of
Catholic conviction
and Jewish fears of
Satan and the Gentile.
Cremation was his answer
to the overwhelming question
of body rot.

Esther
his wife before Tobey
Ron's mother
was long ago buried in a
cemetery beyond his meager means
(at rich Uncle Abe's thoughtless invitation).
She lay unvisited for years on end
because of his fear of being caught
deliquent in the yearly rent.
Tired of skulking around the grassy graves
Harry eventually gave up his visitation rights.

Why, it's a wonder they
didn't dig the poor dear up
and throw her right into the street!
So we called Vitali's Funeral Home on Mulberry Street.
For three hundred dollars cash
they picked up Harry in his own limo
and took the Jew to the oven.
Three days later came the call
"Come pick Harry's ashes up."
Ron sits on the D train with Harry,
heavy in a shoebox
in a brown paper Bloomingdale's bag.
Flustered,
we hide the Bloomie's bag upstairs
and try to forget about it.

Act II: A Night At the Opera

I wake up to the sounds
of a frantic tremulo:
"Oh-oh-oh-ow-ow-ow-oo
Oh-h-h-h-oww-ooo-ooo!"
His jaw jutting forward
his neck tilted back on the pillow
tendons taught
it's Ron howling:
Oh-oh-oh-ow-ow-ooo-ooo!
Unable to sleep
I shake the howler awake
only to stare into his wild eyes.
"Mio Dio, mio Dio
he wants to drag me to Hell with him!"
Ron cries in a deep basso.
"Who? Where?"
"La Commandatore!

Harry La Commandatore
is coming after me.
He's Don Giovanni
on his black night mare!
He jumps off his sepulcher,
there's lightning, fire, brimstone smoke
he's grabbing me
dragging me down to Hell!
I sing to the Don:
'Non, non, non
I don't want to go'.
But with Harry La Commandatore's
eyes flashing
his anger so consuming
I'm helpless."
"Ron, your singing's gonna wake the baby.
Go back to sleep."
The rest of the night is a quiet intermezzo.

The second night:
"Oh-oh-oh-ow-ow-ooo-ooo!"
Harry La Commandatore is back
with Ron Giovanni singing his protests.
After shaking awake the trembling tenor
I go back to sleep.

The third night again
the fourth, the fifth
this interminable opera continues
with Harry terrorizing his son
in death as he did in life.
Death does not always you part.

Next weekend
Naoko, our Japanese babysitter arrives
asking politely "How are you?"
Too tired to simulate wellness
the story pours forth.
Now Naoko is no stranger to death.
Her family being heirs to Hiroshima
she knows from afterlife protocols.
Shaking her head grimly
lips tight
she asks deadly serious:
"Where your fodder's bone buried?"
"Umm-mm....we didn't,
 he's upstairs in the Bloomie's Bag."
Her horrified expression gives us the answer
"You must bury your fodder as you promised,
 or his ghost will live here forever
 and come to you every night."
That does it.
The next day, we make the arrangements.

Act III: The Burial

Me, Pearly, Tobey, Ron,
and two-year-old Emma,
are squeezed into the "mommy car"
my little green 1981 Honda
in which my mother's ghost has lived since 1983
the year she died.
It's 1992 now
and we are driving to Mount Hebron cemetery
to bury Harry
his "bones" in the trunk
in the brown paper Bloomie's bag.

It's an old crowded cemetery
full of Jews and Armenians
persecuted minority outsiders
at last on their own turf
in this mostly Italian and Irish part of Queens.
The oldest sections are way in the back
in far distant corners
against the old crumbling ten foot high wall
that keeps the Jews in their ghetto.
The roads are narrow here
former footpaths with lots of dead ends.
Our car navigates around old granite tombstones
tall and leaning
some inlaid with fading portraits in
tarnished brass oval frames.
Round stones sit on top.

We pile out of the car
Pearly's got Harry
"Boy, he's heavy."
Tobey with a small spade
and a red potted geranium
is orange-haired seventy
wearing black stretch pants
with sling back sandals.
Rhinestones glint on Pearly's cat eye glasses.
"Take off your rings so you don't get dirt in them."
I grab Emma's hand
to wander off down the road
ostensibly to stand guard.
It is illegal to bury someone in
someone else's grave.
They are afraid of discovery by the
cemetery guards,

which seems to be a chronic condition
of Barnetts in cemeteries.
Ron Giovanni sits in the car,
his face hiding in shadows.

Bored
Emma and I play hide and seek
amongst the gravestones
until I loose her in the spaces in between.
Panicked
fearing her fallen into a hole eight feet deep
I call her name
my voice turning soprano
as I jump over and over mounds
running faster and faster.
Tired, smiling
I find her sitting on the edge of a granite slab.
Happy to have her small hand in mine
we walk back.

Ron has been called out of the car
Tobey's arthritic spurs making it too painful to dig.
Now three big round bottoms
brown, beige, and black
over leather souls
are facing the sun like
open flowers gently swaying.
The first ill-fated shovel thrust
hits Elenore's box with a clack
so all three in unison
like a dark centipede
move together to the right
further down the grave.
Yiska prayers said

the deed is sealed with the
red geranium deeply embedded in the soil.
("Let's hope the gardeners here
don't pull it out. They're very strict.)
Sweating, they scurry back to the car
which I drive backwards
down the path to the world of the living.

On the road out
a huge flock of crows flows overhead
to land on an old oak tree,
sitting there
like ripe black fruit.
These crows are family to me.
They were here when we buried Mama
here when we buried Daddy
here when we buried Grandma
here when we buried Ralph.
These crows are the descendants of crows
that have watched my family's descendants
descend into their graves for generations.
They are the Watchers.

The road winds up and down around
in curves as we get lost trying to exit.
Emma throws up on Pearly.
It's the best thing that's happened all day.
When we reach the big black wrought iron gates
Ron, sotto voce, says:
"When I die, don't spend any money on a funeral.
Just cremate me."

HAIR

White wisps of hair fall into my lap
as I get my hair cut.
Looking in the mirror
I realize that once I had feared turning into my mother.
Now I am turning into my grandmother.
I rub some hair between my fingers
feeling its age.
Again the snip of scissors around my ears.

I have an old yellowed envelope filled with
gentle curls of chestnut brown hair.
My mother saved the tresses cut off by Regina
my friend who lived above us on the second floor.
We were six and playing hairdresser.
My mother was hysterical.
My curls never grew back
but not for want of trying.

Wrought iron curling tongs
like medieval instruments of torture
rest in the gas flame.
Mother waits until they are almost red hot.
I sit on the yellow vinyl chair
head back on the edge of my mother's kitchen stove
throat exposed
waiting to have my hair curled.
I see the green ivy on yellow lattice wallpaper
the three bulbs glowing on the ceiling.
I hear the song from the street
   "Buy old clothes!
      Buy old clothes!"
as the used clothing peddler pulls his wooden cart
with two long poles
large wooden wheels creaking.
He is his own horse.

The huge pile of dark blues, blacks, browns
natural cottons, wools, camel's hair coats, pants, dresses
is sorted through by neighbors
bought and traded.
The fibers look earthy
are deep to the touch
swell when wet with the rain.
Standing crowded together in the subway
during rush hour every morning,
on my way to school,
deftly avoiding an errant hand,
I could smell the animal in the damp fibers
the lingering odor of human sweat in a woolly coat.

And once again,
leaning forward,
he slowly pulls away singing:
    "Buy old clothes!
      Buy old clothes!"

I feel a wet tug on my scalp.
The room fills with the acrid smell of burning hair
as mother curls the strands around the sizzling iron.
Again and again all around my head she works
pulling and turning.

My hair thoroughly cooked
she says "Sit up"
and
I run to the mirror—
my whole head is full of
dark fusilli curls falling in round layers.
Now I love my mother.
Now I can dream the lonely romantic dreams
of a ten-year-old girl.

I'M LOOKING OVER A FOUR-LEAF CLOVER

My front lawn in Maltby
is covered in huge green three-leafed clovers.
I wander through them barefoot
amazed at their size
their coolness.
I am tempted to fall down on my knees
and crawl around
to look for those that have four leaves.

To a three-year-old child even small clovers look huge
as I hunt in the grass in Alley Pond Park
my father sitting nearby on a wooden bench
staring into space for hours on a Saturday morning.
He asked me to find him a four-leaf clover
"for good luck."
What went through his mind all those hours
his face blank?
I never thought to ask.
Children don't question the staring into space of adults.
I spent those hours diligently on my knees
looking through thousands of three-leafed
not-this-ones,
looking for the I-found-it.

I don't know much about my father.
Everything I do know is a reflection
of his relationship to me.
He was an unknown man.

I once found his name
on a yellowed sheet of onion skin paper,
a letter of reference from an umbrella company
dated 1929.
The unknown man sold umbrellas in Europe.

"Mein Gott, those Czech soldiers'
boots stank when they took them off at night!"

The unknown man fought on the axis side in World War I.

He and his sisters
my Aunts Elsie and Selma
owned a dressmaking business in Vienna.
The unknown man sold dresses in Europe.

Then, in Queens, NY, in 1945
at the age of fifty-five
the unknown man became known as my father
and that's how I met him.

All those hours on that bench
did he remember selling umbrellas
as his three-year-old baby daughter kept looking for luck?
Was he remembering what he left behind
his mind
like mine now
recreating the past
wondering where did it go if it's still here in my head?

I went back to Alley Pond Park
sixty years later with Emma
so she could ride her single speed bicycle
on a track that dated back to the 1939 World's Fair.
Weeds, garbage, overgrown paths, a leaning Port-O-San
the neighborhood had chipped away
at the edges so much that I couldn't find my little pond.
How much more beautiful was the memory
than the present reality.
Only the cemetery where my father is buried
stays the same.
But then it's supposed to.

My father had a crocodile skin wallet
that my mother brought back for him
from the Belgian Congo in 1951.
Opening it
I slowly turn over stale plastic pages
frosted, and scratched
filled with wrinkled deckled edged photographs
of the most important people of his life:

My young mother, smiling
blond curly hair brushed back
beautiful before they left Vienna.

Hillary, a toddler, holding herself up
on the dark blue couch
in the corner of mother's living room.

Three-year-old Peggy
finger in my mouth
back up against a flowered
wallpaper I don't remember.
Those laced shoes I wore
were once bronzed
with a photo of a naked baby above.
They sat on the tall mahogany dresser for years.
When I left home mother threw them away.

Erika, sixteen
brown hair perfectly curled around her neck.

I had heard talk of a girlfriend in Hungary
before the second war.
This must be Fritzi standing against a broken brick wall
bundled in a dark overcoat
handbag hanging.

Fritzi again with a small white dog
bare armed in the springtime
sitting on a bench one leg up
back against the picnic table.

A black and white pig
no, two pigs, one in shadow.

And a green four-leaf clover
still pressed between.

MEDITATION ON A LOST CAT

At night I hear the tic-tic-tic of his nails on the wooden floor
his shadow passes through a reflected light.
His soul hovers at the door
which I did not open to let him in
in time.
A small life
self-involved
always touching, touching
to say I am here
to say you are here
we exist
no more is necessary.
If I could only hold onto that thought
I could move myself on
through the night
and not keep waiting for the tic-tic-tic of his nails.

There is a tap-tap-tap that is beyond human
a universal touch on my lips
that wakes me up in the early morning
that accepts getting up and washing your face
without doubt.
As I get older
I question less
the search for meanings gets weaker
more tiresome.
I'm evolving into a small soul
relieved to not need answers anymore.
But the why of it
stays with me tap-tap-tap on my shoulder.

My garden's dark soil has no more dig-dig-dig for slugs
not even an orange body to bury.
Gone into the thin air

I breathe in his last life outside
in the winter cold
inhaling my lost warmth.
I watch the trees sway
the wet green grass turn brown
accepting the lesson of my aloneness.
It's only a cat
and it's only a little life
but it's the same life that we all share that's out there
surrounding us and through us.
I have my own allotment for a while until
eventually
it becomes time to dig-dig-dig for me.

DINNER WITH MR. K

It's dinnertime in my mother's kitchen.
The smell of frying garlic
fills the apartment all
the way to the bedrooms.
Sitting at the rectangular yellow
formica table with crumbs in the cracks
my sister and I watch
as Mama makes fun of Daddy's
boiled fish and potatoes
cooked by himself
for the safety of his gall bladder.
The rest of the family stuffs itself on
weiner schnitzel
crepes and roast duck.
His culinary world collides
with my Grandma's Viennese cusine.

"Velcome, Bienvenue! Welcome!"
It's time for "Dinner with Kafka!"
See the occasional Joseph K.
crawling on the wall
"more family come to visit" says my mother.
We sit in a circle waiting
staring
silent before the storm.
I hold my breath.
Suddenly Mama pecks at Papa
he squawks back and
slaps the table with his beak
the room erupting
a flock of crows pecking over crusts
the fork thrown down
the fish gone cold
Daddy flaps away

through the dark doorway
to the living room.
I watch the empty chair
not breathing till he's gone.
"Now eat!" I'm told.

SNOW FALLING ON SPERM

The blizzard blows into my eyes as I lean my shoulder
into the white wind roaring down Lexington Avenue.
With every step my boots disappear into two feet of snow
melting cold over their edges.
My arms curve forward
to protect my children kept warm in an oven mitt
stuffed under my armpit
a little jar of sperm on its way to the lab
there to be counted:
this many alive
this many dead
this many morbidly deformed.
I trudge along.

The sudden heat of the lab dampens my face.
Taking out the jar I put it on her desk.
"That's $300 cash, no check, no credit card."
"There's a blizzard out there!"
"Cash only."
I turn to go out again into the blizzard to the
nearest cash machine.
I see her put the jar on the radiator.
I walk out
hoping to be back before my children come to a boil.

I am thirty-six when we consult Dr. Drucker.
He hands Ron a plastic jar,
"Please give me a sample."
Three days later he tells us
"You don't have enough healthy sperm to have children.
Let me experiment on you, please.
We'll use horse testosterone."
We decline.
We wait

and wait.
I turn forty. Ron turns forty-five.

We then consult Dr. Seltzer.
He hands Ron a plastic jar,
"Mr. Barnett, we need a sample."
Thus the present expedition to the lab at the North Pole
the snow falling on sperm
skyscrapers around me pale and white
at their craggy mountainous summits.
The next day I pick up the sad results of the sperm count.
It's 1985 with handwritten results.
I take a pen of the same color
and falsify the data:
5.5 million turns into 55.5 million.
"There are 55.5 million sperm per milliliter,"said Dr. Seltzer.
"That's not enough.
Morbidity is poor."
It seems many of our children are dead.
"Why don't you try artificial insemination?"

We consult Dr. Idant.
His lab stores semen for future use in frozen vats.
He finds donor matches.
He shows us Polaroids of possible fathers
with a special folder for Orthodox Jews that
guarantees semen from a kosher home.
His phone rings incessantly with calls from his broker,
"Sell GE, buy Bell Labs, sell IBM."
Concentration of sperm is possible.
No guarantees of future life.
He places a little plastic jar on the table.
"Give me a sample, Mr. Barnett."
The sample room has white french shutters.

Ron enters.
He exits five minutes later without the jar and
goes immediately to the men's room to wash his hands.
"There are five college boys in there donating for $25 each.
We're leaving."

Dr. Seltzer starts us on a very experimental regimen.
There are three different hormone injections every two days.
One hormone is extracted from
the urine of post menopausal Italian nuns.
One is luteinizing hormone.
One is synthesized gonadotropic growth hormone.
A nurse trains me to give him three shots a week
three times a week.
Week after week.
Month after month.
I really get tired of sticking those two pink butt beach balls.
I bring little plastic jars to the lab
spring, summer, winter, fall.
Rain, sun, wind, snow Ron is like the post office
always delivering.

The hormones affect Ron dramatically.
He develops huge oily pimples.
He flies into testosterone fueled Raging Bull rages.
After a year the sperm count begins to rise.
His lust is insatiable.
I'm forty-one and I'm still not pregnant.
I learn that during copulation
beer is alkaline and helps female sperm go further
egg white is protein and helps male sperm go further.
I stand on my head after
do deep knee bends before.
Ron is an orangutan grinding his teeth.
The second year is consumed in fire.

One night I awake to a vibration in my abdomen
a gentle trembling.
I go back to sleep.
Two weeks later I throw up.

On the night of July 4th
holding my new baby daughter in my arms
I sit by the huge hospital windows watching fireworks
over the East River.
I see the colors reflect into her eyes and light up her face.
One of the huge rockets goes as high as the sky
bursting into a huge floating ball
of thousands of small golden comets.
Each has a little tail and swims in circles
fiery sperm of life
that fall slowly to earth like snow
and melt.

GINGER SNAP

I was jogging down the road
when her dog bit me in the butt.
A collie with an undifferentiated protective streak
Ginger was nonetheless adored by her mistress.
Her husband volunteered to have the dog put down.
I had the distinct feeling that he
fed up with the biting canine
wanted me to say "yes."
But I just couldn't do it,
couldn't do that to her owner.
When she died
he kept the dog.

MY BLUE JAY

My neighbor's dog gnaws
on the bottom of the drainpipe of my house.

A bluejay built a nest for his female
at the top of that drainpipe
just under the eave
out of the way of rain and wind
but right above my deck chair.
A big lovely twiggy frizzy haired ball of a nest
he worked on it for days
back and forth
the female watching, hopping up and down
on the newly green vine maple nearby.
I had just cleaned the deck of dried winter moss.
He was annoying me
dropping twigs everywhere
yelling at me for being in his way.
I was stuck between sentiment
and wanting to get rid of it.
The annoyance of lice, mites, bird droppings
the rotten black mess of nest falling down
from the roof last winter
overcame my generous reluctance.
The white twelve foot long PVC plumbing pipe
swept it away into the rhododendrons below.
I cleaned the deck again.

The next morning
cappuccino in hand
I sit down on my chair
noting the clean empty space above.
I look down to the right.
On the deck next to me
at the base of the drainpipe

is a shattered blue shelled egg
the yolk soft and runny.

That damn dog is still gnawing on my drainpipe.

SERIOUSLY CEREUS

My Night Blooming Cereus bloomed last night.
I was sleeping and I missed it.
This morning it hung there pink and flacid
obscene
smelling faintly of sweat.
I missed observing its erect state.
Is once a year really too much too ask?

THE TERRARIUM

The soil in my terrarium is dying.
The old fishbowl sits on the ledge of my kitchen window
looking brown and wrinkled.
It got scorched once in New York
and has never fully recovered.
It was in the window that faced the World Trade Center.
Now a few wilted grassy leaves
and mossy swirls climb up the inside
while crumbly brown cracks shrink away from the glass.
I don't want it to die.
I don't want to loose my Catskill memories.

2008

Emma and I are driving through the Catskills
on the New York State Thruway
We're going to Saratoga to visit Tobey
who is now ninety-three.
On the way
we take the Peekskill exit to the Red Ranch Motel.
It's still there
each generation dutifully caring for the clean rooms
stuck in time.
I have just flown 3,000 miles from Maltby, Washington
to fill up a bag with earth from the rocky stream behind it.
I can't use any other kind of soil.
It would grow the wrong memories.

1998

We are in the Catskills.
Emma, ten, with a shovel and Ron
walk to the rocky stream behind our motel
returning with a big plastic bag
full of plants, bugs and earth for a large fishbowl

110

to start a terrarium on the round white coffee table
in her bedroom in Manhattan.
We bring home memories of Pete Seeger
playing his banjo as we drive down winding
mountain roads in the twilight.
When she is twelve I teach her to drive
in one of the many empty weed grown parking lots
that line the road.
Each day we drive her to the Bailiwick Horse Ranch
to learn to ride
a peculiar passion in a city living child.
Ron hits a huge racoon and bends the fender
of the sea green 1981 Honda "mommycar."
We are our family with
Emma always with us in the back seat.
I see her face in the rear view mirror
her bright eyes meet mine.

1957

We are driving to the Catskills.
There is no Thruway yet.
Driving up Route 9W
("Do you spell your name with
a 'V' Herr Wagner?"
"Nein, W")
after singing
over and over again
 "George Washington Bridge"
to the tune of "When You Are In Love"
while crossing the Hudson over a breathtaking span
the river shining beneath us
after stopping at the Red Apple Rest
to eat huge greasy french fries

after my mother drives her black and cream 1957 Ford Victoria
for interminable hours
we arrive finally at Round Hill Lodge
back to Vienna, 1900 in the Catskills.
Emperor Franz Joseph
would be right at home here.
("Now there was a man!")
as Grandma
born in 1881 during the Hapsburg era
always said.
Here the Kaiser's protocols endure.
Life proceeds in an orderly procession of meals.

8:00am
Fully dressed
we eat "Gabelfrustick"
Breakfast Eaten with a Fork.
Shirred eggs, cheeses, ham
creamed herring with raw onion
sweet rolls, sliced pumpernickel
honey, butter curls on ice, strawberry jam
a soft boiled egg
rapped three times with the edge of a silver spoon
oozing soft yellow.
Waiters run
huge round black trays float above our heads.
My heavy silver knife never touches the table
a crisp white, linen napkin on my lap.

12:30 pm
Shorts permitted
a full lunch
of ham. cheese, wiener schnitzel and cucumber salad

with sweet lemon dressing
distends stomachs
the adults take a nap
I, thirteen years old
go look for the pool boy, Freddie, sixteen.
We're alone in the pool.
He's carrying me in his arms.
I lie there horizontally across his
tanned chest, floating.
I know he's going to kiss me.
I panic.
I begin to turn like a chicken on a spit,
over and over
around and around
until reach the edge of the pool
and hang there gasping.
We look at each other.
There are no words for our confusion.
I pull myself out of the water
and run up to my room.
My grandmother sleeps
as I sit on the edge of my bed
wet
feeling my urges.

4:00 pm
is the coffee hour.
Speaking German
the card players eat vanilla cake
strudel, and coffee thickened with whipped cream
soft and sweet, light brown tinted edges
running over the top of the cup.
Short, bald Sascha tunes his violin.
He plays a melange of gypsy sighs,

trills of laughter, lilting rythmns
from a pre-world war one century
when everyone was assimilated.
Manicured, beringed, spoon tinkling fingers
some of which have been pressed into
the wooden slates of catttle cars
slowly lift crumbly yellow bites of cake
to wrinkled red lips.
Perfume floats on the smell of coffee.
Chairs scrape.
The hotel owner
very discretely gay Mr. Burman, smiles
as Sacha plays a waltz.
But Mr. Burman doesn't allow the one armed lady
to dance with the two armed lady.
"Same sex dancing isn't proper." he says.
I guess he means in public.

7:00 pm
I go upstairs to dress formally for dinner.
Every year our hotel room gets smaller
and further up the stairs.
At first it was on the ground floor with a sitting area
a flowered couch and roses in a crystal vase on the table
large french windows opened onto a patio.
In our last years there
we are up two flight of stairs.
Grandma can barely climb them.
There's a slanted dormer roof over the beds
and a sink in the gray room.
We pay extra to use the air-conditioner.
My mother only comes up on weekends
working in her sweltering factory during the week.
I put on a purple rayon dress that feels like silk

blue ribbons on the sleeves
a birthday gift from Mrs. Jellinek.
I feel rich
the way only a child can feel rich,
happy with having one thing at a time
no matter how small.
The oriental carpet scratches my bare feet.
Armed with 47/11 cologne
we descend to the dining room
to songs from "The Merry Widow."
"tripple-tripple-tripple-top!
    tripple-tripple-tripple-top!"
I accept this world as the world
the way the world is, not was.
I forage my way through
chicken soup, goulash
small parsley buttered potaoes
Kaiser rolls and crepes with jam.

After dinner
when it gets dark
my sister slips away to Toro Hill
a place forbidden to me.
Down the road
down the hill
it is a bungalow colony on a small lake
a colony of New Jersey Jews
real American Jews
who only speak English.
I lust to go there.
I imagine all the
grownup goings on down there.
T.V. reception is a blurry grainy black and white screen.
I go to bed.

Years later Round Hill Lodge becomes a gay hotel

and is burned down to the ground by local
religious zealots
living in the decrepit Toro Hill bungalows.
A sacrificial, tribal bonfire
it glowed hot and high in the night on top of Round
Hill.

2008

Having now returned to the Red Ranch Motel
Emma and I swat away huge swarms of mosquitos
as we kneel by the stream in back
digging up moist earth with small ferns.
"This spot here. It's perfect. Damn these mosquitos!"
I had forgotten the mosquitos.
The plastic bag full once more
we run to the car
to continue the drive to Tobey.

The terrarium sits on the window ledge in my kitchen.
As I make my morning coffee
I watch the Catskills grow.
I'm really happy
there are no mosquitos in Maltby.

THE TELEPHONE

I never spoke on the telephone with my father.
I lived with him from the day I was born
until I moved out of the house at the age of nineteen.
I never once spoke with him on the telephone.
Then he died.
The black phone with its noisy, plastic, racheting dial
was always there in the dark foyer of the apartment
on one of grandma's crocheted doilies
on the brown wooden credenza
which opened into a desk
containing odd bits of paper, pennies, broken poker chips
and an ancient roll of clear scotch tape
that always tore a useless ragged piece.
Was he unable to speak into a telephone
because he was born in 1891?
Or was it just that it was my mother's phone.

He never had much to say to me anyway
being in his own mind
in his own bedroom.
That bedroom had a luxury—
a private bathroom
the man's toilet in a house of women.
It had peach colored walls and a peach tiled shower.
A stropping leather for his razor hung from the towel rack
with a brown porcelain cup, brush and shaving soap
kept on the black tile window sill.

I'm two years old.
I love to watch Daddy pee into the toilet.
I stand next to him looking up.
I see his hand holding a big soft finger that sticks out of his pants.
I don't have one.
The pink finger has a hole in it.
Then suddenly the water comes out of the hole
in a long yellow arc frothing into the toilet water
a splendid musty smelling waterfall

a wonder of life.
I stand there mesmerized
until it ends in spurts
then
shaking his finger
Daddy hides it back in his pants.
He pulls the shiny handle and the water roars.

One day I follow him as usual
through the dark bedroom to the bathroom.
This time he turns in the doorway
barring my entry.
I look up at him
a tall, gaunt sillouette against the peach colored light
"You can't come in here to watch me make pee-pee.
Mommy says it's not right for a little girl to look."
He shuts the door in my face.
I stood looking at the sudden blackness in front of me
knowing a terrible loss
of an indefinable love.
My mother was to blame
she the judge
he the executioner.

He never concerned himself with my life any further
so there never really was any reason
to speak on the telephone with him.
He came of a generation that grew up without one
and
he would never dream of answering my mother's phone.

THE DOLL

The fragile pieces are in an old white box—
a leg
pink arms
(some with hands attached,
pointy fingers curled towards the palm)
a porcelain torso.
Curly straw colored hair frames round blue eyes
staring up at me.
The twine that connected all the parts
has long rotted away.
This doll belonged to my mother-in-law-the-child.
Lavender scented smoke rises when I move the tissues.
I feel her hovering over me
watching.

Esther died forty two years ago but
I don't think she passed over all the way.
There is rumored to be a space
between this life and the next
where you remain if you refuse to move on.
It's like the dark space between the adjacent walls
of my dining room and my bedroom.
She visits us in the evenings on this side of beyond.
She makes Ron scrub the spotless stovetop every night.
The water runs in the kitchen sink for hours
pounding on porcelain
reeking of bleach.
Sometimes I see ectoplasm emerge from Ron's mouth
in the form of a clean white terry cloth towel
for him to use to dust the living room.
Sometimes she slinks back into that half place
where transparent arms try to grab her
and drag her resisting spirit over there.
But there's too much dirt left behind here
for her to go away
the cleaning of which killed her
as she claimed it would.

She never took her coat off when sitting in my home
her pink fingers wrapped in scotch tape
to keep the edges of red detergent cracks together.
The older Ron gets
the weaker is his will to resist.
We are now living with her.

This doll
her baby
is broken.
It needs a doll doctor.
New twine will make it whole.
In her box I gently cover those staring blue eyes
with a white tissue paper shroud.

THEY'RE DROPPING LIKE FLIES

They're dropping like flies around here.
There are three on the slider rail of the living room window
legs up.
They're behind the heart-shaped pathos leaves on the floor
in the corner.
Six are on the mudroom mat behind the yet-dry winter shoes.
I used to find one or two every five years or so
then one every two years.
Now they're everywhere I turn
black bodies
bluish shells reflecting the sky.
First the flies were outside.
Then they got in
found the front door, I guess.
They bump against the glass
of the windows in the kitchen
trying to get out.
Bump, bump, bump
buzz, buzz, and bump.
The glass is a trap.
Looking out one can see the world
alive
growing
resilient
energy with a future.
But they'll never get out now.

Behind the window here in the corner
behind the rocking chair
another fly just dropped.

PARADISE VALLEY TRAIL

Dripping interrupts the tall silence as
I walk alone on this forest path
seeing gold rain on arabesques of fern
deep twisted space between red vine maples
huge yellow leaves spotted brown.
Drops of cold water hit my hand.
A lonely wind blows against my face
moving the leaves to applaud my solitary mood.
Spongy moss moves softly north on hemlock bark
overgrowing its compass.
A gray speckled stone egg is half buried in fir needles.

My college has an old surveying camp
that city living art students use
to study landscape painting
a form that came naturally to 19th century artists
but seems to have been lost among
the tyrannical abstractions of our times.
I've had a bad day painting in the snow.
My feet are frozen
the bright glare on icy pools
doesn't translate easily onto canvas.
I've dragged tubes of oil paint, brushes, and turpentine
here on an endless bus ride through New Jersey back roads.
I live in an old wooden house
sleep in a bunk bed with a gray, old wool army blanket
that smells of someone's sweaty flannel shirt.
I'm not Cezanne in Provence.
Leaving the communal kitchen that winter night
full of a cheap hot tuna casserole
prepared by the painting teacher
who has three fingers missing on her right hand
I enter the dark clear night to cross the land home to my bed.

It's cold.
The crescent moon sits low.
Shadows curve around shiny white mounds.
Pines are black holes.
I look up.
Stars are sharp and shiny.
I lie down on my back on the snow
which envelopes me with
a dead lover's cold arms.
I sink deeper into the warmth
as I look up into ancient eyes.
I hear a slithering in the snow.
Death chills my bones.
Thrilled, I tremble into
an orgasm of the night.
I fall asleep in his arms.

Startled, I awake in the dark and cry:
"Go, wild bone man!
Leave me, my love!
I'm still young!"
Death hisses:
"Then when?"

Over the years Death and I meet occasionally,
tentatively
one night of love in the snow binding us.
"Are you ready?"
"Not yet."
The last time we met we quarreled.
Arguing with Death is exhausting.
"Are you ready?"
"I do feel a little tired."
"I'll wait."

I keep walking alone on the trail

enveloped by cold mist.
Ahead of me on the gnarly path
a snake has slithered through the mud
leaving moist wavy lines.

LEAVING LOVE

To truly know love
you have to leave it
see it grow smaller behind you.

People seem so much kinder
less demanding when they are about to be gone.
The embrace is warmer
more true
if there is even the vaguest chance
that it will never happen again.
You hug
not face to face
but chest to chest
with hearts beating
arms aligned in circles.
You know that the time for arguing has passed.

Quiet words
laughing acknowledgment of reality.
We all know the truth
that underneath it all
love is always the way it is
that's just the way it is.

We wave good-bye.
I say "I love you" to the wind.

ABOUT THE AUTHOR

Peggy Barnett was born in 1945 in Queens, New York. She worked as a professional still-life photographer in Manhattan for 40 years. She moved to Washington State in 2006. Country life has given her the time to contemplate the memories that have formed the patterns of her life. She can be contacted at onyourleft@mindspring.com and her website can be viewed at prbarnett.com

ACKNOWLEDGMENTS

Thank you to the editors of the following journals in which these poems first appear, sometimes in slightly different form:

Quillandparchment.com, "If You Love Me."

Sundial Press LLC, " Gnarled Roots, " "Leaving Love" and "Meditation on a Lost Cat" in *Gatherings and Gleanings*.

Terry Busch for editing this book and making my poetry more poetic.

My sister Erika Michael. When I arrived here from New York six years ago she generously introduced me to the world of Northwest Poetry and to her friends poetic.

My husband Ron who has had to sit through many poetry readings that revealed some pretty personal issues. He has done it with grace and humour.

My daughter Emma for her love and support of my writing and for designing this beautiful book.

The poets of Washington State who made me feel so welcome and a little bit exotic. I salute the dedicated poets who lead and manage the many venues at which I have had the pleasure and honor to read. They are the steadfast engineers that drive the train of poetry in the Northwest.